My Store in [the Mall]

Understanding Percents

Dawn McMillan

Publishing Credits

Editor
Sara Johnson

Editorial Director
Dona Herweck Rice

Editor-in-Chief
Sharon Coan, M.S.Ed.

Creative Director
Lee Aucoin

Publisher
Rachelle Cracchiolo, M.S.Ed.

Image Credits

The authors and publisher would like to gratefully credit or acknowledge the following for permission to reproduce copyright material: cover Shutterstock; p.1 Getty Images/Tanya Constantine; p.4 Corbis/Matthias Tunge; p.6 Corbis/Patrick Durand; p.7 Shutterstock; p.8 (both) Big Stock Photo; p.9 (left) Shutterstock; p.9 (right) Pearson Education/Alice McBroom; p.10 (top) Alamy, (bottom) Shutterstock; p.11 Alamy/Jacky Parker; p.12 Shutterstock; p.13 Big Stock Photo; p.14 Shutterstock; p.15 Alamy/Neil Setchfield; p.16 Photolibrary.com; p.17 Island of the Blue Dolphins cover reproduced with permission of Penguin Books UK; p.18 Corbis/Ludovic Maisan; p.19 Alamy/Jeff Greenberg; p.20 (left) Getty Images; p.20 (right) Getty Images/Tanya Constantine; p.21 Pearson Education/Alice McBroom; p.22 Getty Images/Ross Anderson; p.25 Getty Images/Stephen Derr; p.26 Getty Images/ Tanya Constantine; p.27 Alamy/Jim West; pp.28–29 Shutterstock

While every care has been taken to trace and acknowledge copyright, the publishers tender their apologies for any accidental infringement where copyright has proved untraceable. They would be pleased to come to a suitable arrangement with the rightful owner in each case.

Teacher Created Materials

5301 Oceanus Drive
Huntington Beach, CA 92649-1030
http://www.tcmpub.com
ISBN 978-0-7439-0909-9
© 2009 Teacher Created Materials, Inc.
Reprinted 2012

Table of Contents

My Store

This is my store. Feel free to take a look around and see if there is anything you would like to buy. Most people think of my store as just a bookstore, but I also sell **stationery** (STAY-shuh-nair-ee), gifts, toys, and cards. So come on in!

Busy places like malls and airports have bookstores.

My store used to be much smaller than it is today. Two years ago, the store next door shut down. I decided to rent that area, too. I knocked down a wall to extend the floor space of my store to 4,090 square feet (380 m²). Now it is 40% larger than it was before.

LET'S EXPLORE MATH

Percent (%) means out of 100. One whole is 100%. The square below represents 1 whole. The whole is divided into 100 equal pieces. 50 pieces are shaded, which means that 50% of the whole square is shaded.

Percentages may be **converted** (con-VER-tehd) to fractions and decimals. So, 50% is 50 out of 100 or $^{50}/_{100}$ or 0.5.

The fraction $^{50}/_{100}$ is the same as $^5/_{10}$ or ½. These are known as **equivalent fractions**.

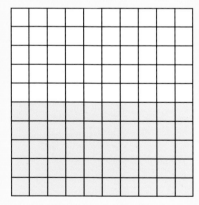

a. Write 25% as a fraction.   **b.** Write 75% as a decimal.

c. How many pieces of the whole would be shaded to show 60%?

5

A bigger store means that I have to pay more rent. But the extra **revenue** (REV-uh-new) I earn covers the cost of the higher rent.

I also had to buy new carpet and store **fittings** for the whole area. It cost me $140,000 to extend the store. The new shelves cost $16,000. The big glass window in the front of the store cost $22,000. But it was worth every penny! Now I can create exciting book displays in the window. People passing by really notice my displays.

Some store owners hire people to make window displays.

Inside My Store

The items that are for sale in my store are called stock. My store has an area for each kind of stock—books, magazines, stationery and cards, gifts, and games and puzzles.

Some of the floor space in my store is for books and magazines. At least 20% of the floor space is for adult fiction. At least 20% is adult nonfiction, and 8% is children's books. About 2% of the space is used for magazines.

Use of Store Floor Space

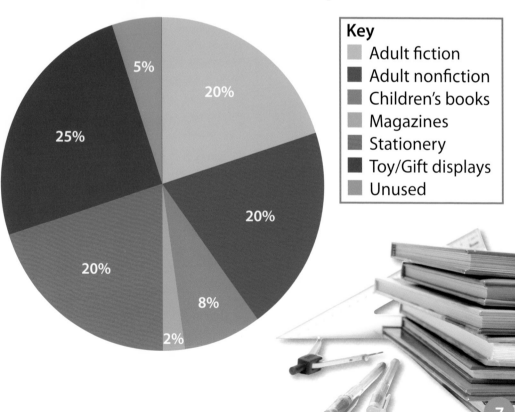

Key
- Adult fiction
- Adult nonfiction
- Children's books
- Magazines
- Stationery
- Toy/Gift displays
- Unused

5%

20%

25%

20%

20%

8%

2%

About 20% of my store is stationery. This means $\frac{1}{5}$ of the store floor space is filled with cards, paper, pens, journals, and notepads. I also have school notebooks, pencil cases, and cool school bags!

Bright colors and patterns attract people's attention.

Before I extended the floor space of the store, I sold fewer gift items. Now, toy and gift displays use 25% of the store floor space.

LET'S EXPLORE MATH

In the store, 50% of the floor space is used for books and magazines, 20% is used for stationery, and 25% is used for toy and gift displays.

a. Write 20% as a fraction and a decimal.

b. Write 25% as a decimal.

c. What percentage of the floor space is not used?

d. If the floor space of the store is 380 m², how many square meters of floor space do the books and magazines take up?

I need to save some floor space for seasonal stock. Seasonal stock is stock that people only buy at certain times of the year. For example, I sell gifts for holidays. I also sell cards for special occasions (oh-CAY-shuhns). In the month of December, I sell gift wrap and holiday cards.

There is no wasted space in my store. I use the walls to display stock. Even the counter area displays games and puzzles.

Colorful wrapping paper is very popular during the holiday season.

How My Store Works

My business is in retail, so I am called a retailer (REE-tail-er). A retailer sells goods for people to use. Many retailers have stores on the streets or in shopping malls.

This bookstore is in a shopping mall.

Some retailers do not have stores. They sell their stock online over the Internet. Customers can order things by using a computer. Online retailing is called e-commerce.

Online shopping is quick and easy.

E-Commerce

Online shopping is very popular. Many people have busy lives. They have no time to shop at stores. People can buy what they need online without having to leave their homes.

I buy my stock in large quantities (KWON-tuh-tees) from wholesalers. A wholesaler buys stock from the company that makes the items—the manufacturer (man-yuh-FAK-cher-er). The wholesaler buys the items at a lower price and then sells them to retailers like me.

The retailer then sells single items or small quantities of an item to the customers. The customers are called the end users. This is because they are the last people to buy the stock. The customers do not sell the item to anyone else.

LET'S EXPLORE MATH

The store has 200 packs of trading cards to sell. On Monday, 10% were sold. By Friday, 80% of the total stock had been sold. On Saturday, the store sold another 20 packs.

a. How many packs of trading cards were sold on Monday?

b. By Friday, how many packs of trading cards were sold in total?

c. How many packs of trading cards are left at the end of the day on Saturday?

Pricing My Stock

The price I pay for my stock is called the wholesale price. The retail price is the price paid by the customers. I have a formula for figuring out the retail price for my stock. This is my price formula: Retail Price = Wholesale Price x 2.25.

I round the retail price up or down. For example, if the retail price of a stock item worked out to $3.04, I would sell it for $2.99. If the retail price was $37.67, I would sell it for $39.99. I could make it $40.00, but $39.99 sounds much cheaper!

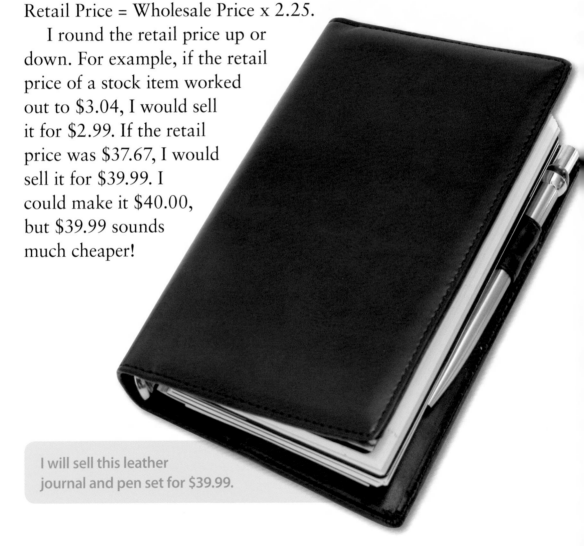

I will sell this leather journal and pen set for $39.99.

The difference between the wholesale price and the retail price is called my mark-up. My mark-up helps pay for things like the store rent, advertising, bills, and **salaries** (SAL-uh-rees). After I pay all these costs, I hope to have some money left over. This money is my **profit**. I **deposit** it in the bank until I need it.

Many store owners go to the bank every day.

The more of a stock item I buy from the wholesaler, the cheaper that stock item is. So, if I buy 1 pack of 24 pencils, the wholesaler charges me 10¢ per pencil. But if I buy 5 packs of 24 pencils, the wholesaler only charges me 8¢ per pencil. The cheaper wholesale price is a reward for buying more stock.

Although I buy packs of pencils, I sell each pencil separately in my store.

Chain Stores

Some stores can get an even cheaper cost price from wholesalers. This might be because the stores are part of a **chain**. Chain stores are stores that are all owned by the same big company. They all have the same name, stock, and prices.

Sometimes a chain store has a single owner who **leases** the **brand name** from the big company. This kind of store is called a franchise (FRAN-chize).

Any type of store can become a chain or franchise.

LET'S EXPLORE MATH

A survey asked 400 franchise owners about the type of franchise they own: 50% had grocery stores; 25% had bookstores; 20% had toy stores; and 5% had other types of stores. Use this information to figure out what fraction of the owners have these franchises:

a. bookstores

c. toy stores

b. grocery stores

d. other stores

Chain stores can buy stock from wholesalers at a very cheap price. This is because all the stores can join together and place one really big order. The larger the order, the cheaper the wholesale price.

Chain stores use a pricing formula too. So, a cheaper wholesale price means a cheaper retail price for customers. It's hard for me to compete with big chain stores! This is because I cannot purchase as much stock as they can.

Forklifts move big orders of stock.

Pricing Books

I do not use my pricing formula to price the books in my store. Instead, the retail price is decided by the **publisher** of the books. In this case, the price is called the **recommended** (REK-uh-MEN-ded) retail price (RRP). The publisher gives me a **discount** on the RRP, and that decides my wholesale price.

For example, a publisher decides the RRP of a children's book is $14.95. That means the book will cost customers $14.95 in all bookstores. But the publisher gives me a 40% discount when I purchase it. Each book costs me only $9.00.

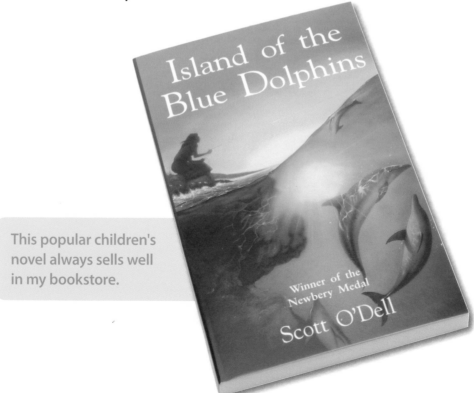

This popular children's novel always sells well in my bookstore.

Marketing My Stock

As a retailer, I need to market my stock. To do this, I need to find out what my customers want. Then I figure out a way to sell it and make a profit. Marketing includes pricing, advertising, and displaying the stock in my store.

Marketing helps sell books. In spring, I make a special display using gardening books.

Part of my marketing plan is to have sales. During sales, I give some stock items special low prices. Special prices are only low for a short time. The special prices attract customers to the store. If customers know that a certain item is cheaper at my store, they will shop here first. Then they might buy more items, even if those items do not have special prices.

Sale days are really busy days in my store.

People crowd around a sale table outside a bookstore.

LET'S EXPLORE MATH

A retailer adds a percentage onto the wholesale cost of an item before it is sold. For example, if a retailer buys a journal from the wholesaler for $15.00 and adds on 20%, the journal will sell for $18.00.

20% = .20, so .20 of $15 = $3.00. $15.00 + $3.00 = $18.00.

Round these wholesale costs to the nearest dollar, then find the retail price of these items:

a. journal: $19.99 + 10% mark up *Hint*: 10% = .10

b. pen set: $23.99 + 25% mark up *Hint*: 25% = .25

c. stationary set: $29.99 + 50% mark up *Hint*: 50% = .50

More Sales

This time of year is one of the busiest for my kind of store. Summer vacation is nearly over. A new school year is about to start. I want customers to buy all their new books and stationery from me, so I am having a "5 Days Only!" sale. I am offering 25% off notebooks, 15% off pens, and 20% off all colored pencils.

Many stores have special sales at back-to-school time.

This week, I will put some holiday wrapping paper rolls on sale. The holidays were over months ago, so I need to get rid of them. The wrapping paper is $5.99 per roll, but I have reduced the original price by 30%. I hope the lower price will get customers to buy them.

$5.99 round to $6.00
30% = .30

.30 x $6.00 = $1.80

That means the discount is $1.80.

Now, subtract the discount from the total to find the sale price.

$6.00 – $1.80 = $4.20

The sale price is $4.20 per roll.

Many shoppers look for bargains just after the holiday season is over.

My Business Plan

The total stock in my store is worth $250,000. My total revenue is about $1.2 million per year.

I use the money I make from selling stock to buy new stock. I have other expenses, too. I have to pay the salaries of my staff. I also pay $120,000 a year in rent. And my marketing costs are 4% of the total revenue.

I use my computer to keep track of my stock and my store costs.

I have **sales targets** for each month. The targets are part of my business plan. The targets depend on the time of year. During busy times, my sales targets are higher. These targets help to keep me working hard. And hard work makes my business a success!

Sales for 2008

Month	Target Sales	Actual Sales
January	$90,000	$85,000
February	$100,000	$105,000
March	$110,000	$100,000
April	$110,000	$110,000
May	$120,000	$125,000
June	$150,000	$160,000
July	$150,000	$150,000
August	$120,000	$135,000
September	$100,000	$100,000
October	$100,000	$85,000
November	$150,000	$140,000
December	$180,000	$190,000

Sales targets are part of my budget. A budget is a plan that shows how much money I hope to earn and how much money I need to spend. I make a budget for each month. I follow my budget so that I do not spend more than I earn.

Monthly Budget—February

Income	
Books	$55,000
Magazines	$20,000
Gifts	$25,000
Other	$5,000
Total income	**$105,000**
Expenses	
Rent	$10,000
Salaries	$12,000
Marketing	$400
New stock	$10,000
Other	$7,000
Total expenses	**$39,400**

Profit: $105,000 − $39,400 = $65,600

Good Service

When my store first opened, I worked very long hours. Getting the store set up took a long time, but it was worth it. Now my store has a good **reputation** (rep-yoo-TAY-shuhn) in the local area.

These days, I only work weekdays. I have some great **employees**. They run the store on weekends and when I am on vacation.

Choosing employees carefully is very important.

I am happy being a retailer, but it is very hard work. My store is open from 8:30 A.M. to 5:30 P.M., 7 days a week. I am on my feet all day. But I love talking to customers and helping them find what they need. It is a very rewarding job!

Some customers like to **browse** before choosing a book.

LET'S EXPLORE MATH

The bookstore is having a sale: children's books are 50% off retail price, adult fiction books are 25% off retail price, and cookbooks are 10% off retail price.

To find the sale price, you need to work out how much the percentage off discount is and then subtract that from the original price. For example, a children's book retails at $24.50. It is 50% off, or ½ price. So, .50 of $24.50 = $12.25. $24.50 − $12.25 = $12.25.

Round these book prices to the nearest dollar, and find the sale prices of the items below. *Hint*: 50% = .50, 25% = .25, 10% = .10

a. children's book—retail price: $35.50

b. cookbook—retail price: $39.99

c. adult fiction book—retail price $15.60

My Own Chain

I have a new goal. I am going to rent another store in a nearby town. I will have two stores. That means I will be a chain!

I am busy planning my new store. Already I am wondering if I will have enough space for my stock. The store next door is empty, so perhaps I will be able to expand my new store right away.

This store will look very different with new fittings!

Books at a Bargain

Jamal has a $100.00 gift card to spend at Bargain Books. Jamal loves reading mystery books. But he also likes books about different countries and cultures. And Jamal wants to learn to surf!

Jamal would also like to buy his family some books. His younger sister enjoys adventure stories. His dad enjoys cooking, and his mom loves gardening and fashion. Bargain Books is having a big sale. Jamal has chosen 8 books that he really wants to buy.

MICKEY'S WORLD TRAVEL ADVENTURES

Retail Price: $59.90
Now 25% off

SURFING FOR BEGINNERS

Retail Price: $29.75
Now 20% off

COOKING WITH LOUEY

Retail Price: $48.25
Now 25% off

The Adventures of Pirate Mouse

Retail Price: $19.50
Now 10% off

exploring **France**

Retail Price: $35.50
Now ½ price

Mystery of the Cherry Orchard

Retail Price: $16.20
Now 75% off

Greenthumbs Gardening

Retail Price: $22.00
Now ½ price

Fashion Designing

Retail Price: $42.80
Now 25% off

Solve It!

a. How much money would Jamal spend if he bought all 8 books on sale?

b. Unfortunately, Jamal has only a $100 gift card to spend. Decide which books Jamal would buy if he had to choose, and give reasons for your choices. Think about the books he and his family like.

Use the steps below to help you work out your answers.

Step 1: Round each book price to the nearest dollar.

Step 2: Find the discounted amount for each book.

Step 3: Find the sale price of each book.

Step 4: Calculate the total sale price of all the books.

Step 5: Now decide which books Jamal could buy with his $100.00 gift card. Give reasons for your choices.

Glossary

brand name—a name that identifies a seller's goods or services

browse—to inspect a book or other goods without hurry

chain—a group of stores that share a brand name

converted—changed from one form to another

deposit—to put in a bank for safe keeping

discount—the difference between the regular price and a sale price

employees—people who work for pay

equivalent fractions—fractions that have the same value or amount; fractions that are equal

fittings—objects that can be removed from a property without damaging it

leases—rents out for money

profit—the difference between the earnings and expenses of a business

publisher—a person or company that produces the work of an author

recommended—advised that something is worthy and should be accepted

reputation—the opinion people hold about a person, group, or organization

revenue—the total amount of money returned from a business

salaries—money paid regularly to people for working

sales targets—amounts of money or sales someone hopes to make

stationery—writing paper and other desk and office supplies

Index

Let's Explore Math

Page 5:

a. $25\% = \frac{25}{100}$ or $\frac{1}{4}$

b. 0.75

c. 60 pieces

Page 8:

a. $20\% = \frac{20}{100}$ or $\frac{1}{5}$; 0.2

b. $25\% = .25$

c. 5% is not used.

d. 190 m²

Page 11:

a. 20 packs were sold on Monday.

b. 160 packs were sold by Friday.

c. 20 packs are left

Page 15:

a. $25\% = \frac{25}{100} = \frac{1}{4}$ own bookstores

b. $50\% = \frac{50}{100} = \frac{5}{10} = \frac{1}{2}$ own grocery stores

c. $20\% = \frac{20}{100} = \frac{1}{5}$ own toy stores

d. $5\% = \frac{5}{100} = \frac{1}{20}$ own other stores

Page 19:

a. $19.99 = $20.00 rounded up
10% = .10, so .10 of $20.00 = $2.00;
$20.00 + $2.00 = $22.00 retail price

b. $23.99 = $24.00 rounded up
25% = .25, so .25 of $24.00 = $6.00;
$24.00 + $6.00 = $30.00 retail price

c. $29.99 = $30.00 rounded up
50% = .50, so .50 of $30.00 = $15.00;
$30.00 + $15.00 = $45.00 retail price

Page 26:

a. $35.50 = $36.00 rounded up
50% = .5, so .50 of $36.00 = $18.00;
$36.00 – $18.00 = $18.00 sale price

b. $39.99 = $40.00 rounded up
10% = .10, so .10 of $40.00 = $4.00;
$40.00 – $4.00 = $36.00 sale price

c. $15.60 = $16.00 rounded up
25% = .25, so .25 of $16.00 = $4.00;
$16.00 – $4.00 = $12.00 sale price

Problem-Solving Activity

a. *Mickey's World Travel Adventures*
25% of $60.00 = $15.00 discounted amount
$60.00 – $15.00 = $45.00 sale price

Surfing for Beginners
20% of $30.00 = $6.00 discounted amount
$30.00 – $6.00 = $24.00 sale price

Cooking with Louey
25% of $48.00 = $12.00 discounted amount
$48.00 – $12.00 = $36.00 sale price

The Adventures of Pirate Mouse
10% of $20.00 = $2.00 discounted amount
$20.00 – $2.00 = $18.00 sale price

Exploring France
50% of $36.00 = $18.00 discounted amount
$36.00 – $18.00 = $18.00 sale price

Mystery of the Cherry Orchard
75% of $16.00 = $12.00 discounted amount
$16.00 – $12.00 = $4.00 sale price

Greenthumbs Gardening
50% of $22.00 = $11.00 discounted amount
$22.00 – $11.00 = $11.00 sale price

Fashion Designing
25% of $43.00 = $10.75 discounted amount
$43.00 – $10.75 = $32.25 sale price

Total sale price of all 8 books:
$45.00 + $24.00 + $36.00 + $18.00 + $18.00 + $4.00 + $11.00 + $32.25 = $188.25
Jamal would spend $188.25.

b. Answers will vary.